LEARN TO READ WITH PHONICS

Dear parents and teachers,

This is a fast and effective way of teaching your child to read fluently, whether he or she is:

- four and ready to read,
- a reluctant reader aged nine or more,
- if he or she has a learning difficulty,
- or if English is a second language.

This reading scheme is for you.

- It is for everyone who wants to **read fast**.
- This scheme is **easy to use**.
- It uses **phonics** or sounds.

The course consists of eight reading books. Book 1 and 2 are for pre-readers. These teach initial sounds and word building with three or four letter words. Books 3 - 6 teach phonic sounds in this order:

ch, sh, wh, th, oo, ee, ar, or, ur, ir, er, magic e, ea, oa, ai, ay, oi, oy, oa, short y as in happy, long y as in sky, soft c as in mice and soft g as in engine, ou, ow, au and aw.

The final book introduces more complex sounds as in, tion, le, el, prefixes and suffixes.

There are further titles available on our website, for readers who have attained a degree of fluency.

How does it work?

Each chapter introduces a sound.

1. Learn the sound with your child.

2. Read the sentences several times, encouraging your child to talk about the picture.

3. At the end of the sentences, there is a list of words and phrases, which the child can match to the pictures.

Practise each sound several times, until your child is familiar with it.

It is **important** to **practise**. We advise that you move on to the next sound chapter only when you are confident that your child has learnt all the material.

The child works out words, by learning the phonic sounds and then running them together.

ch ee k y

ar ch er y

hun dred - has two syllables

80% of words can be learnt this way, but a few words will need to be learnt by **looking**, **saying** and **remembering** them.

Children using phonics in this way progress fast.

Dear Kids,

Sam

Kim

LEARN TO READ BY READING WITH SAM, KIM AND THEIR FRIENDS.

Meet Sam and his sister Kim.

They have a cat and a dog called Spot.

Next door, there are two children called Frank and Kelly. They are the best friends of Sam and Kim.

You will meet some more of their relatives and friends including: Auntie Grace, Uncle Cyril, their cousins Grace and Nancy, the famous cousin from the country, his mum and dad, and Frank's Uncle Paul, who takes the children out.

You will also meet: Kim's friend Candice, Sam's school friend Peter, who likes football, his teacher and his class mates, like Heather.

Have Fun Learning To Read.

This course may also be used by older children or adults, who have problems with reading and spelling.

Read the sentences, but concentrate on spelling the words in each chapter, progressing from easier to harder words, depending on ability.

It is as easy as that!

If you need help using the scheme, email at:
www.guineapigeducation.co.uk

Sam's dog Spot says, "Learn these words,

snap, spot, slug,

drip, grin, clap,

drum, frog, pram

trot, plot."

Can you spot,
sn, sp, sl, dr, gr,
cl, fr, pr, tr, pl
sounds?

Read these sentences and meet Sam and Kim.

I like to play snap.

Spot is a dog.

Kim has a spot.

Sam grins at his mum.

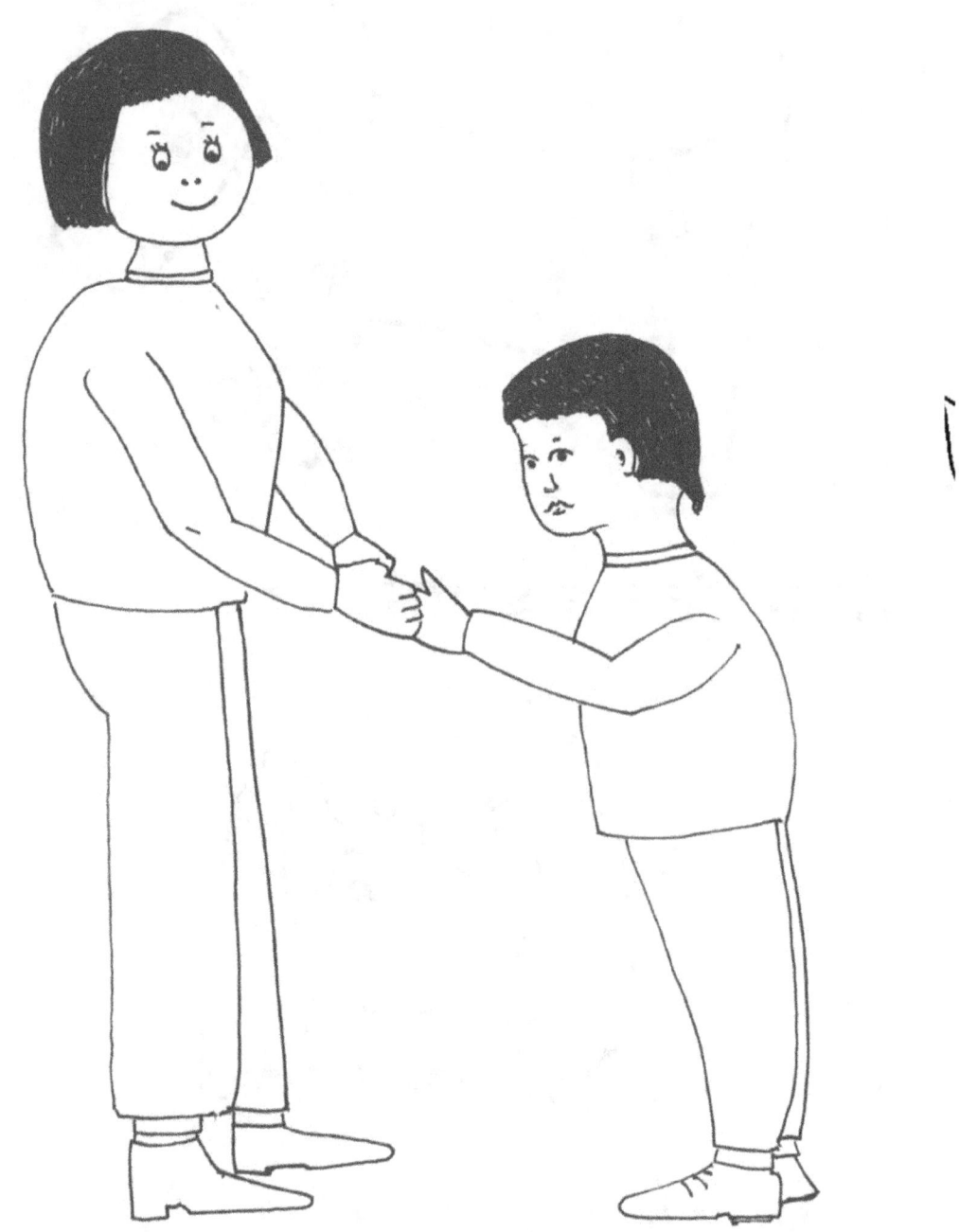

A slug sits on a plant.

Sam claps.

He hits the drum.

I see a frog on the grass.

Kim has a doll in the pram.

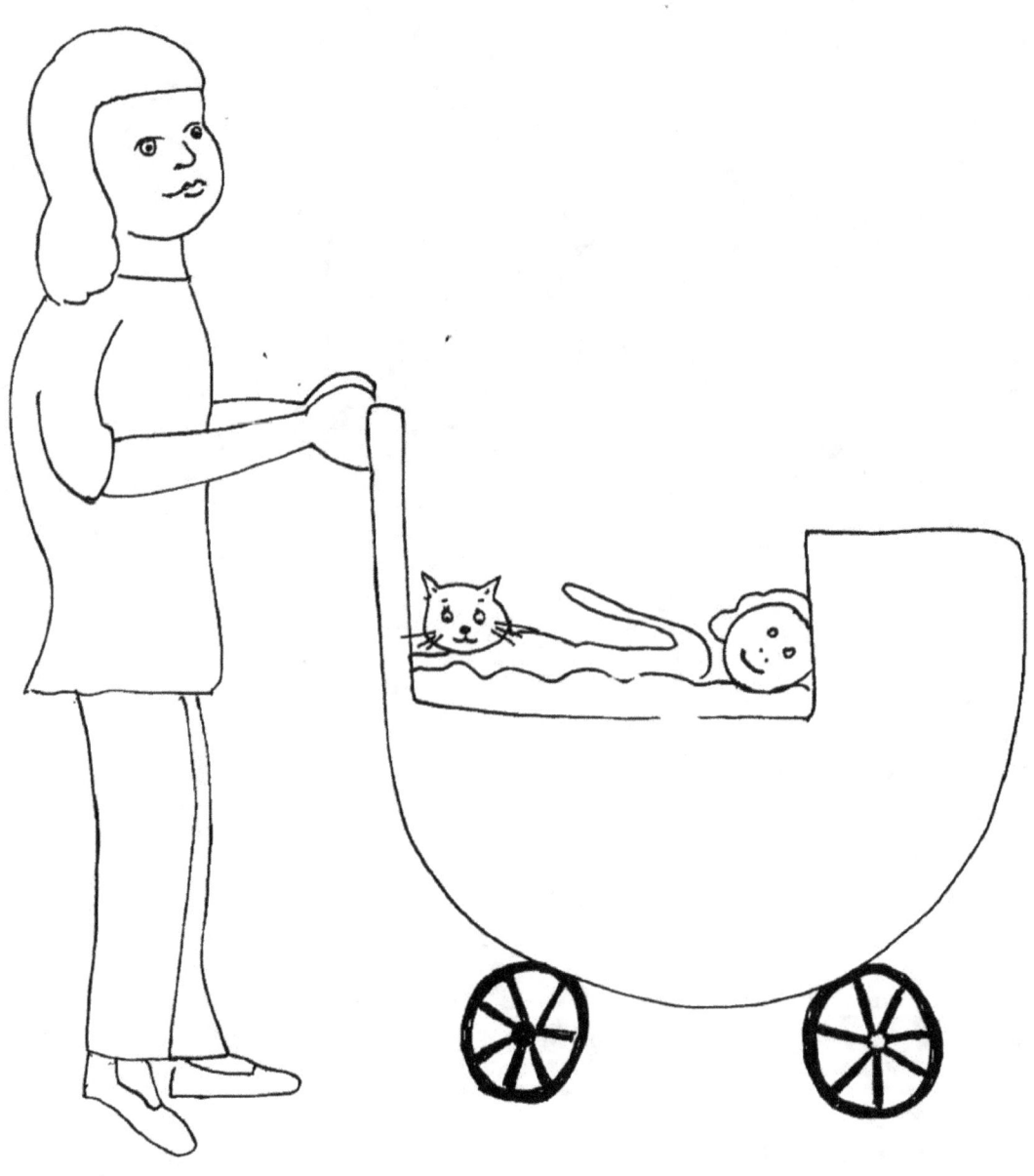

A pig trots.

The tap drips.

Sam's dog sits on a plot of land by the flats.

Cut out these words and make sentences.

Kim	has	a	doll
in	the	pram.	A
pig	trots.	Some	flats
are	going	up	on
a	plot	of	land.
I	see	a	frog
on	the	grass.	

Learn these words. Cut them out and match them to the pictures on the next pages.

grin	trot	snap
spot	plot	drip
flat	slug	clap
drum	frog	pram

If you know these words go onto the next chapter.

Sam's soft cat likes to rest in the sun.

Learn these words…

milk, soft, rest,

hold, hand, belt

himself, myself,

sing, song, crisps,

bank, jump, sank

Read these sentences...

Sam likes milk.

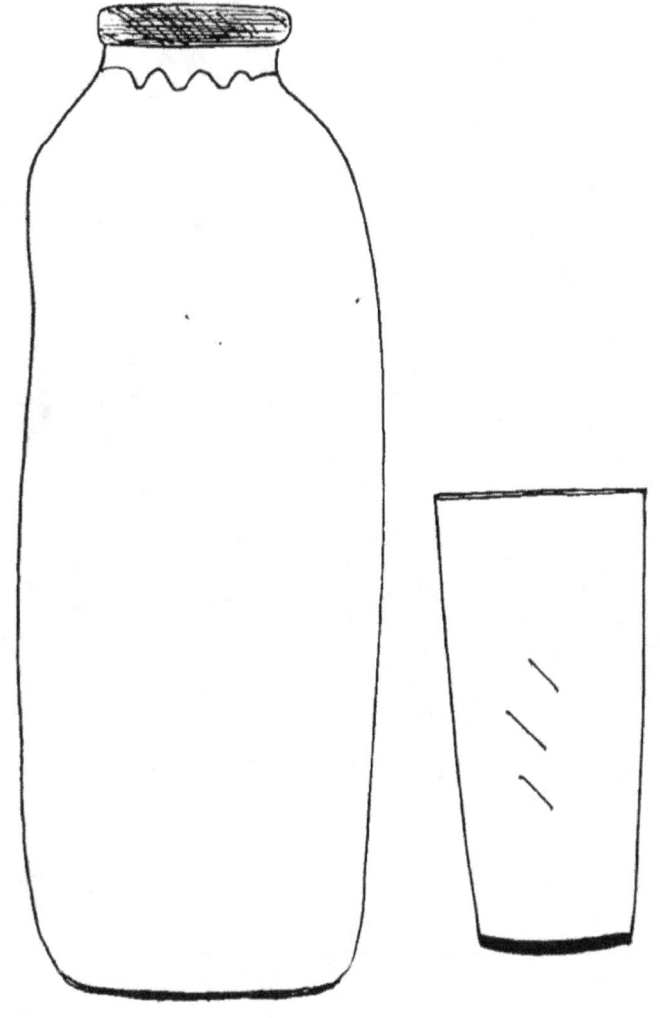

He gets some milk from the shop with his mum.

Sam's cat is soft.

She likes to rest in his bed.

Sam's cat has a rest in Sam's bed.

Sam holds mum's hand.

Sam's mum has a belt.

Sam can draw his hand himself.

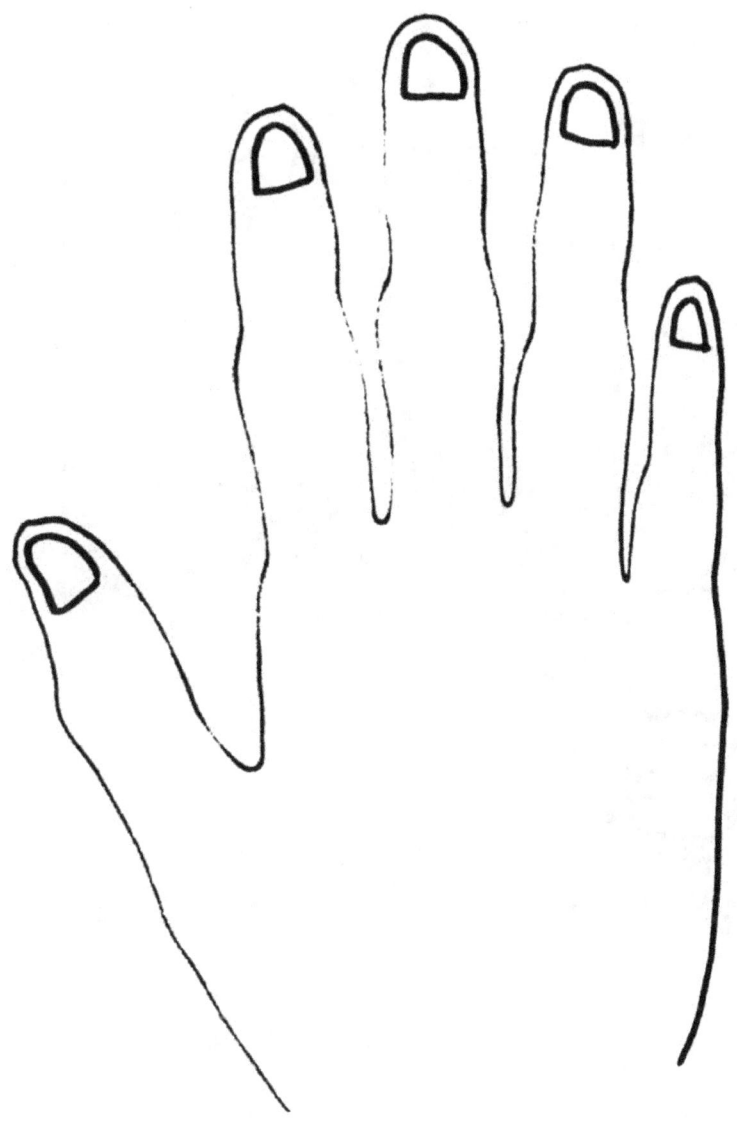

Sam can draw himself.

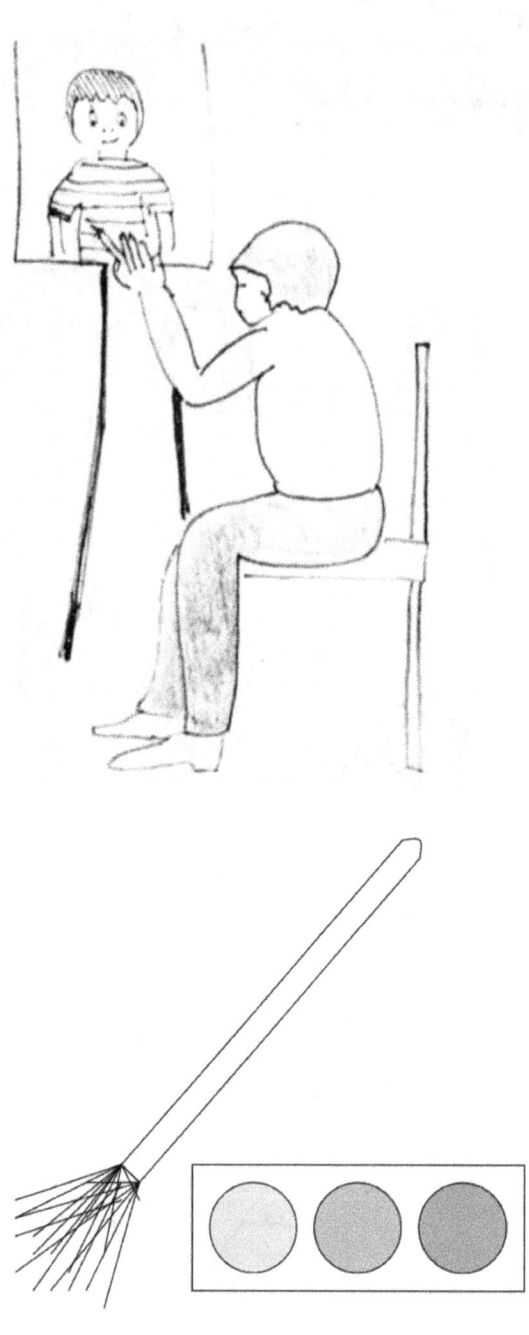

Myself:

He sings a song.

Sam and mum go to the shops to get crisps.

They go to the bank.

Sam can jump.

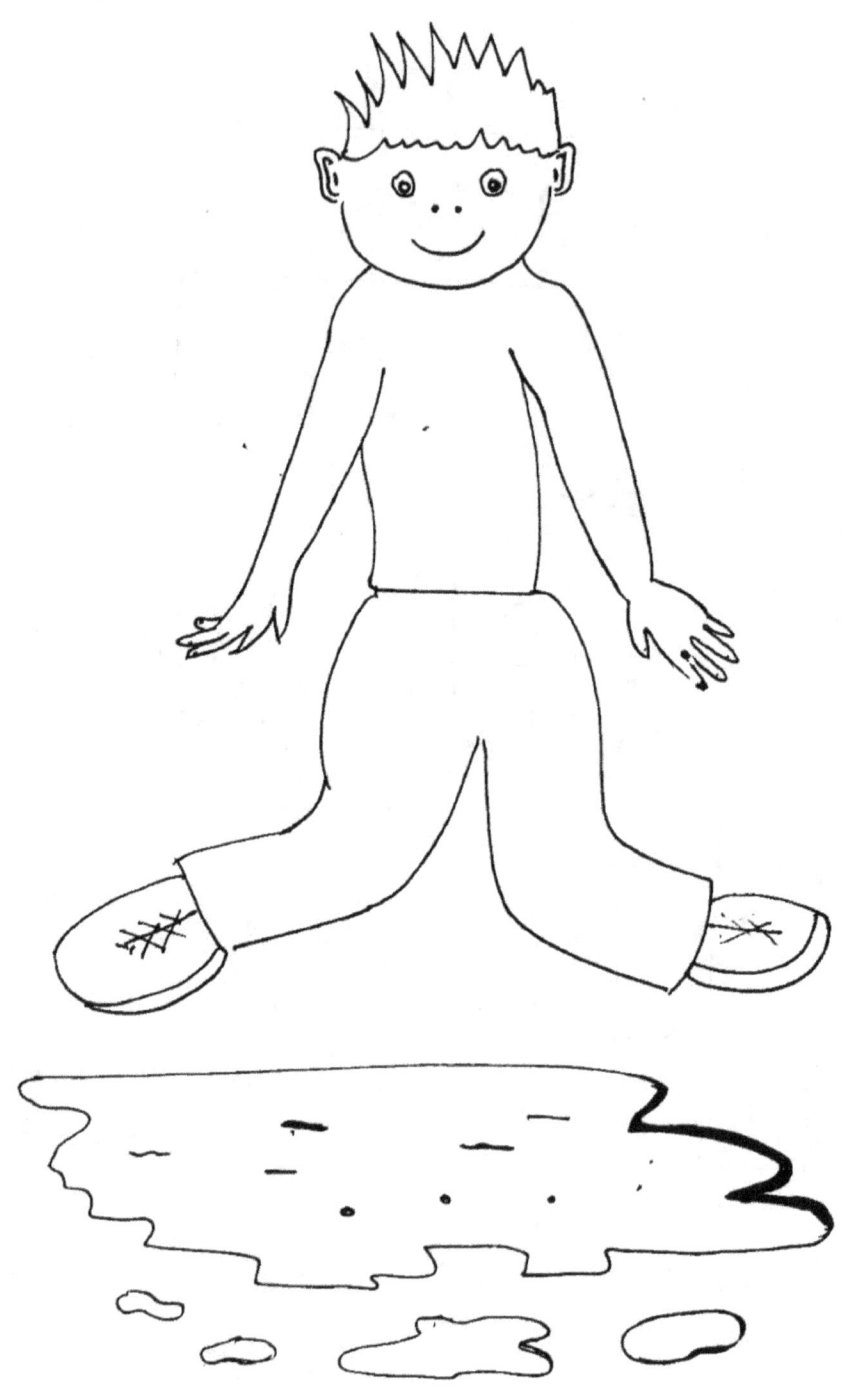

Spot runs to get a stick but it sinks in the pond.

**Spot's stick sank.
Can he get it?**

Learn these words. Cut them out and match them to the pictures on the next pages.

soft	holds	hand
rests	himself	belt
sings	song	jump
shops	crisps	sank
milk	rest	bank

If you know these words go onto the next chapter.

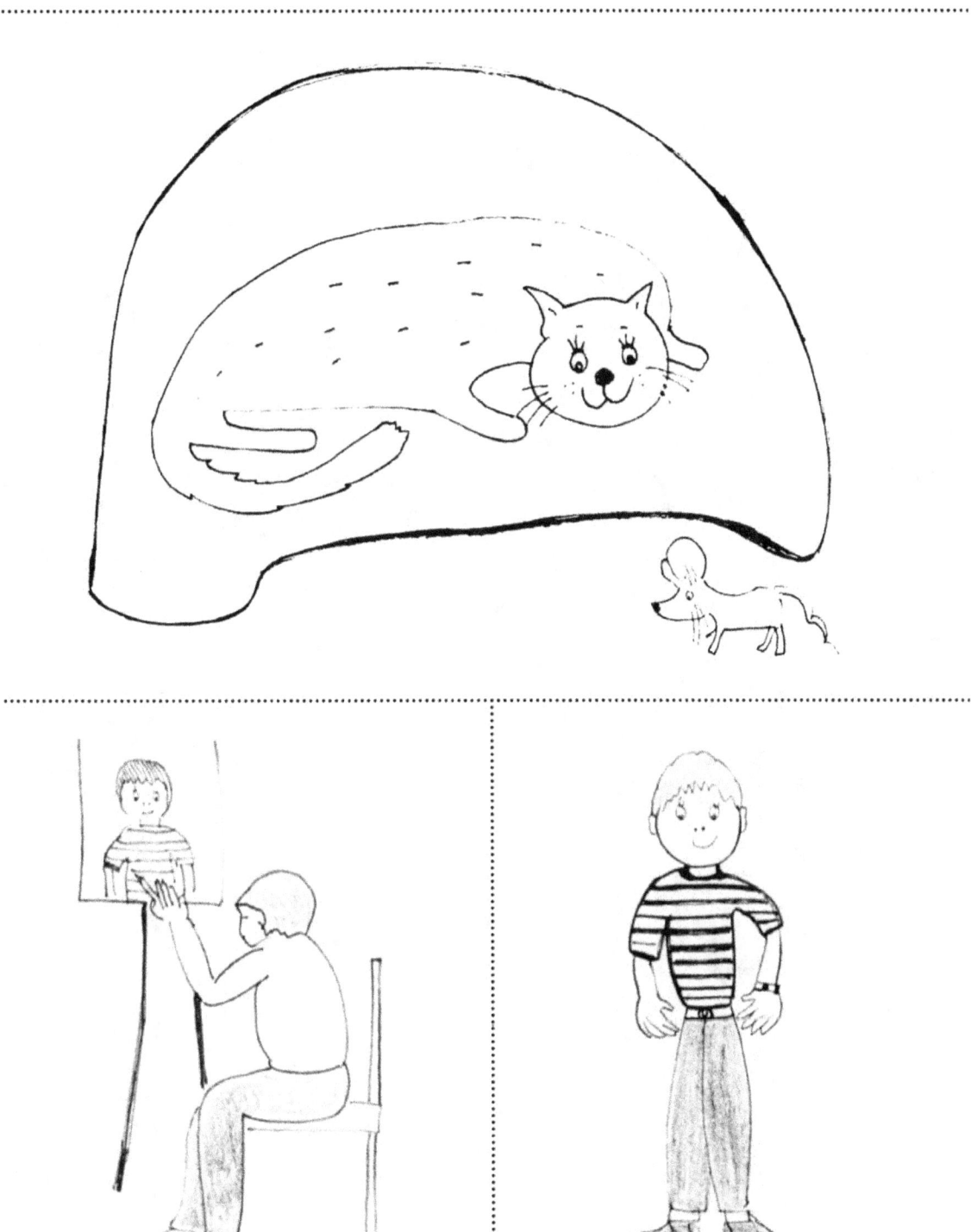

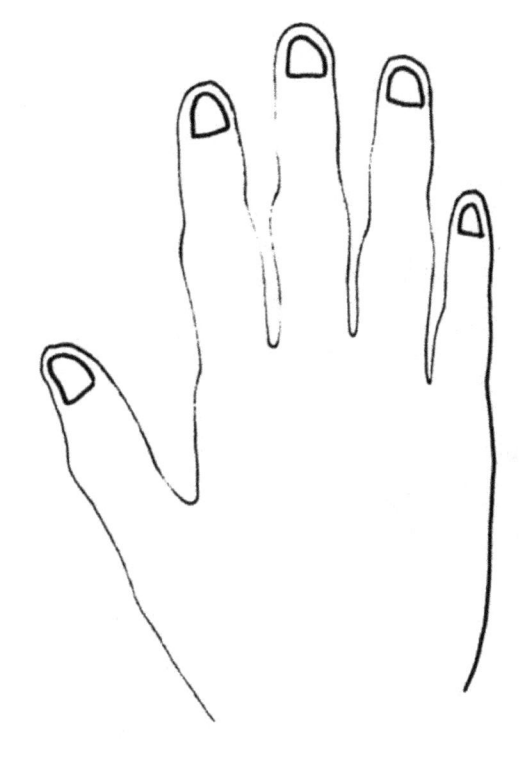

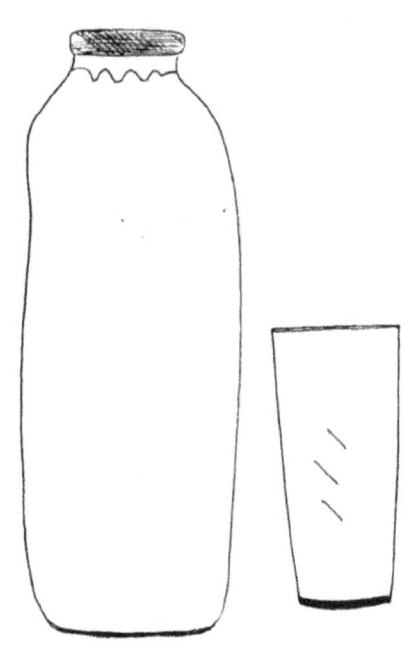

When k is at the end of a word,
   we put a c in front of it.

ck

Read these sentences...

Sam and Kim go to the docks.

They stand on the deck of a ship.

Sam has a
stick of rock.
He licks it.
He sucks it.

Kim sits on
the rocks.
She plays in
the sand.

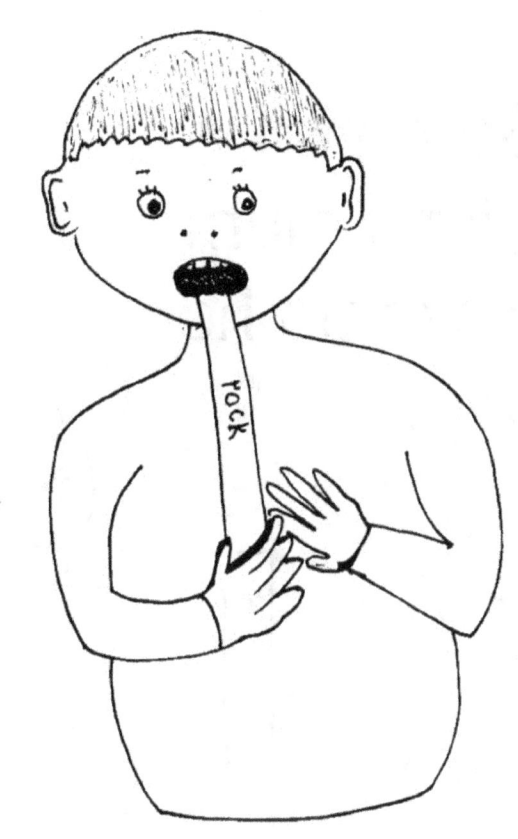

Sam and Kim's mum picks up her bag.

She locks up the house.

The clock ticks on.

They go to the shop. Sam runs back to his house and his mum unpacks a bag.

Kim likes the cat a lot.
The cat licks her hand. It licks her neck. It tickles.

You are a pickle.

Kim likes the duck but it pecks her hand.

Spot the dog kicks up bits of mud. He runs for a stick.

Sam's mum gets a pan off the rack.

> **Learn these words. Cut them out and match them to the pictures on the next pages.**

rock	stick	pack
back	clock	deck
lick	peck	duck
rack	tick	dock
pick up	lock up	kick

If you know these words go onto the next chapter.

Sam's cat with seven kittens helps you read these sentences.

Use the sounds and syllables
to sound out the words,
as in **s ev en**.

Seven has 2 syllables
sev en
The words
lem on and **kitt en**
also have 2 syllables.

Read these sentences…

Sam says, "Let's play the trumpet."

Sam has a drink of lemon in his flask.

Sam has some stamps. He has one hundred stamps.

He runs and jumps.

He jumps from the plank.

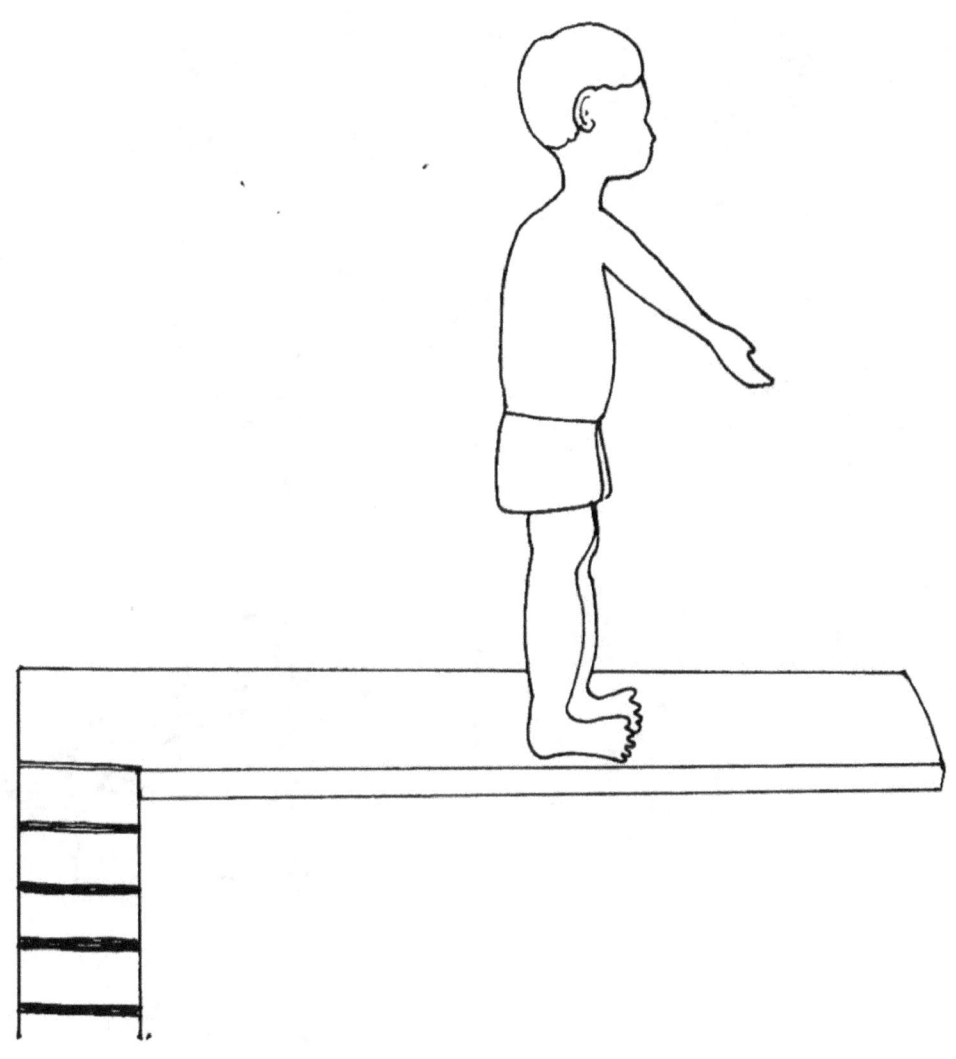

A rabbit is in the run but it cannot get the plants.

Sam has a drink of lemon but the cup is empty.

Sam and Kim play on the swing.

They play on the old tree stump.

Frank likes to get a comic at the shop.

Sam has a sting.

It is nasty for him.

Sam has cramp in his leg.

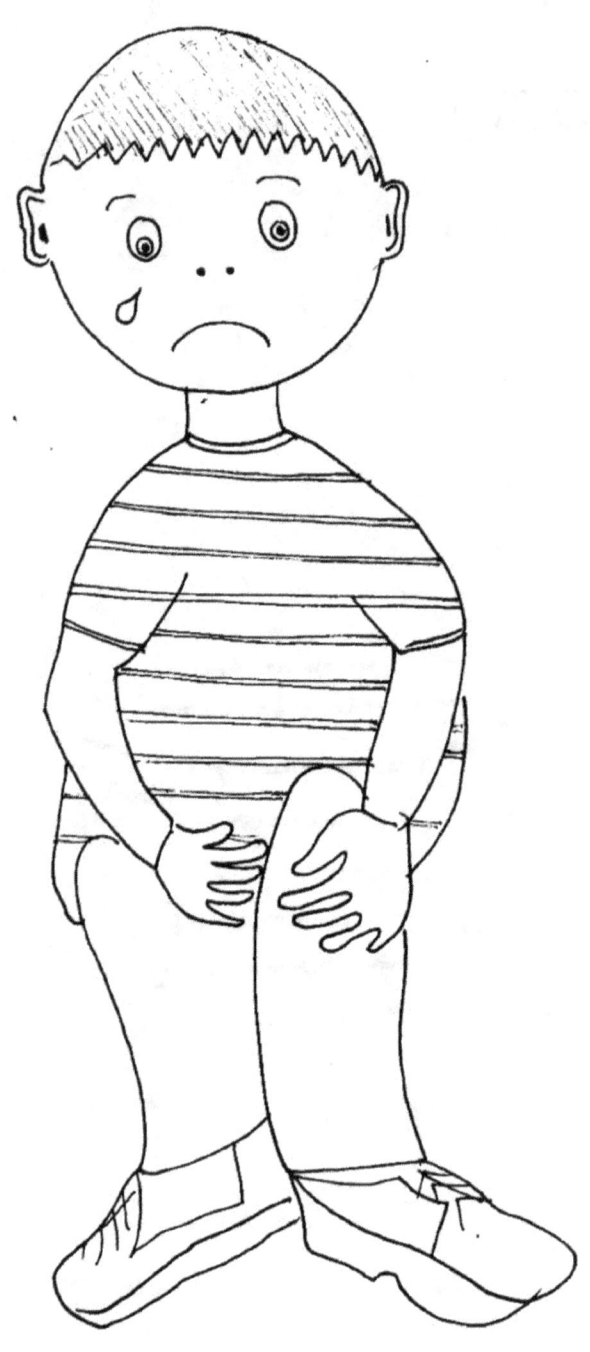

Sam's cat has seven kittens.
A kitten is in the basket.

This kitten is a rascal.

Sam stands on the stump.

Learn these words. Cut them out and match them to the pictures on the next pages.

lemon	empty	Frank	seven
swing	flask	cramp	basket
plant	trumpet	rabbit	sting
hundred	nasty	plank	drink
stamp	stump	comic	kitten
stand	rascal		

If you know these words go onto the next chapter.

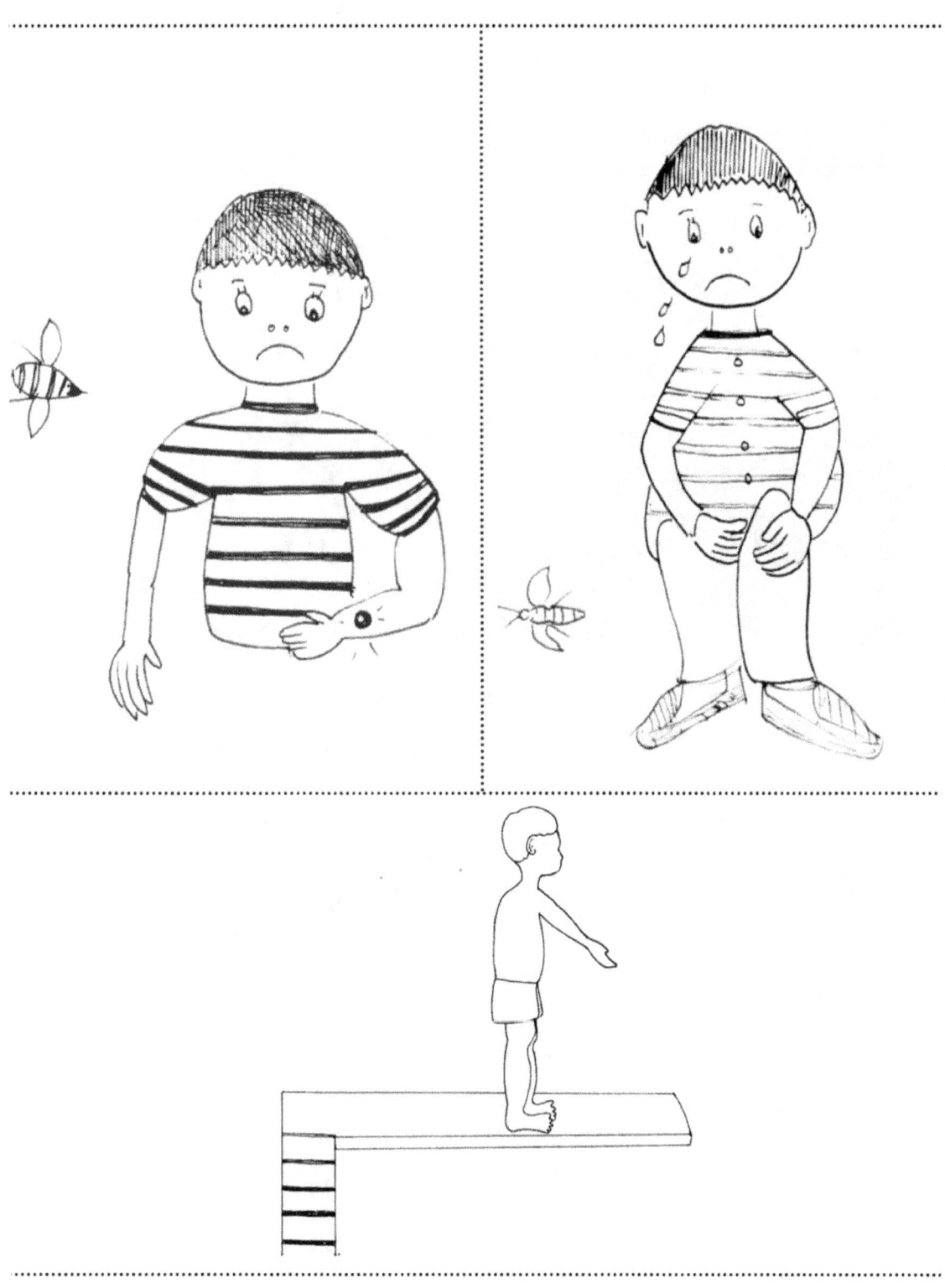

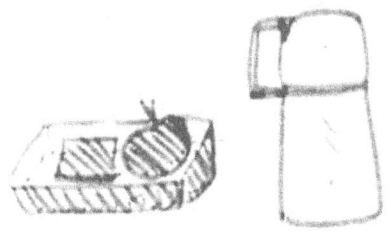

Sally and Amanda Jones

© Copyright 2009

Written by Sally A. Jones and Amanda C. Jones

Published and Printed by GUINEA PIG EDUCATION

2 Cobs Way,
New Haw,
Addlestone, Surrey,
KT15 3AF.
UK.

www.guineapigeducation.co.uk

NO part of this publication may be reproduced, stored or copied for commercial purposes and profit without the prior written permission of the publishers.

ISBN: 978-0-9561150-3-4

Other titles in the Learn To Read With Phonics series include:

Pre-Reader Book 1   ISBN: 978-0-9561150-1-0
Pre-Reader Book 2   ISBN: 978-0-9561150-2-7
Beginner Reader Book 1 ISBN: 978-0-9561150-3-4
Beginner Reader Book 2 ISBN: 978-0-9561150-4-1
Beginner Reader Book 3 ISBN: 978-0-9561150-5-8
Beginner Reader Book 4 ISBN: 978-0-9561150-6-5
Beginner Reader Book 5 ISBN: 978-0-9561150-7-2
Beginner Reader Book 6 ISBN: 978-0-9561150-8-9

www.ingramcontent.com/pod-product-compliance
Lightning Source LLC
Chambersburg PA
CBHW080833010526
44112CB00015B/2505